Romsey's Public Walk and Pleasure Ground

GW00726901

Geoffrey Morris

Published by G. Morris, 32 Church Street, Romsey, Hampshire.

Acknowledgements:

Thanks are due to the Hampshire Record Office, the Romsey local history society (the LTVAS Group) and the Special Collections Department of the Hartley library in Southampton University for providing most of the information that enabled the story of the park land, once known as Romsey's Public Walk and Pleasure Ground, to be pieced together. The Record Office and the Hampshire Field Club kindly gave permission to reproduce the engraving on the front cover and another of the Abbey Church on page 25. The LTVAS Group gave permission to reproduce the remaining pictures from their archives.

Friends and local historians kindly read through the draft and Frank Green, at the time Heritage Officer of Test Valley Borough Council, made additional helpful comments and corrections to the early history of the Public Walk. My good friend, Ted Mason, steered me through the legal bits. Errors or omissions remaining in the book are the responsibility of the author.

Relevant Papers:

Following publication, papers relevant to this book will be lodged with the Hampshire Record Office in collection ref 179A07.

Published in September 2009
© Copyright Geoffrey Morris
ISBN No: 978-0-9563311-0-6
Printed by The Studio, Dukes Mill, Romsey. SO51 8PJ

CONTENTS

Romsey's Public Walk and Pleasure Ground
    – an outline of its story   *1*

1544 – Romsey people buy the Abbey Church   *3*
    and a Processional Way

1773 – The Processional Way is lost but   *5*
    churchwarden Biggs rides to the rescue

1826 – Romsey people buy a Public Walk   *11*
    and Pleasure Ground

1855 – Avery Moore comes to town   *16*
    and builds a new vicarage

1859 – Avery Moore has a problem   *26*
    with his horse and carriage

1875 – Berthon's encounters   *28*
    with the Public Walk

1895 – Cooke Yarborough's concern   *31*

1910 – Another Church claim to the Trust land   *33*

1985 – Another new vicarage   *35*
    but an old access problem

Events around the millennium   *42*
    – the Charity Commission intervenes
    – hearings in Chancery

Romsey's Public Walk and Pleasure Ground
– an outline of its story

Romsey is a cosy old market town that grew up alongside Romsey Abbey on the eastern bank of the River Test; a chalk stream that flows full and clear throughout the seasons. The town is ringed by small villages that separate it from Salisbury, Winchester and Southampton which are all nearby. The Broadlands Estate, once the home of Prime Minister Lord Palmerston, is at its southern edge and the town itself is dominated by the magnificent 12th century Abbey Church which is all that remains of the once proud and prosperous Abbey.

Romsey's Public Walk and Pleasure Ground is the piece of open ground which lies to the west of the Abbey Church. It is bounded by the old vicarage, the new vicarage and the church hall and is about the same size as the town's Market Place. At present, half of it is grassed and the other half, surprisingly for a sensitive part of a conservation area, has been covered with patchwork tarmac and is used as an unregulated public car park.

Romsey's Public Walk (hatched) at the west end of the Abbey Church

In the 1820s, Lord Palmerston noted that the town had no public space for such things as fairs or shows and offered to contribute towards one. In response to this generous offer, Romsey Corporation organised a public appeal to raise the rest of the money needed to buy some land. Most of the land shown hatched in the sketch was purchased and was to be held by the Corporation:

"Upon Trust to permit the said pieces or parcels of ground to be used at all times for ever hereafter as a Public Walk or Pleasure Ground for all peaceable and orderly persons..." (1)

These words, which are found in the conveyances when the land was purchased, are important as they constitute a declaration of a binding Public Trust.

In the 170 years or so that have elapsed since the Trust was set up, the land that it governs has been the subject of many arguments and exchanges between townspeople, the local council and the Church authorities. Trouble started in 1856 when the vicar rather arrogantly built his vicarage on part of it. His attempts to breach the Trust failed after being referred to some of the highest legal authorities in the country. From that time to now, the Church has made a further seven claims to access or own the land. All without any real evidence.

During the 20th century, following the acquisition of the Memorial Park, the Public Walk became forgotten (although the Church claimed ownership of part of it in 1910) but it surfaced again in 1985 when plans for a new vicarage at its western edge were announced. Questions about who owned the adjacent Public Walk and who had the rights over it were raised just as they had been when the Reverend Avery Moore built the first vicarage on its northern edge in 1856.

In the early 1990s, a local resident who was studying the history of Romsey Abbey came across references to Trust land. This led to the formation of a small group of people who wanted to clarify the ownership of the land, the rights of the owners and the status of the Trust. They hoped that their work would lead to the restoration of this small part of the town's lost heritage and promote the enhancement of the area.

In this book, the story of this piece of land begins in 1544 and ends in 2009 following hearings in Chancery triggered by recognition of the Trust by the Charity Commission. Events over this period are well documented (2) and the personalities of some of the more colourful characters involved emerge through their actions and their letters.

1. This is an extract from the conveyances of land from Sharp and Young to Romsey Corporation dated 1st and 2nd December 1826.
2. Copies of most of the papers relating to the history of the Public Walk are lodged with the Hampshire Record Office in Winchester ref: 179A07.

1544 – Romsey people buy the Abbey Church and a Processional Way

The town loses its monastery

Because much of Romsey's Public Walk and Pleasure Ground is land that originally lay within the walls of Romsey Abbey, we have to look back to

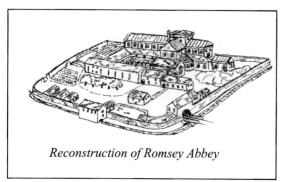

Reconstruction of Romsey Abbey

that time to tell the whole of its story. The Abbey was one of the larger monasteries in the country, but by the time of the Dissolution it had been in decline for many years and its number of occupants had dwindled to the

Abbess and 25 sisters. Henry VIII's reasons for closing down the monasteries are arguable but the need to top up the coffers of the Treasury was certainly a driving force among some of the people concerned. Henry's chief minister, Thomas Cromwell, had previously reported on nearly every monastery in the country and had concluded that:

"manifest sin, vicious, carnal and abominable living is daily used and committed among the little and small abbeys".

This allegation helped Henry to present his Suppression Act of 1536 as an act of reformation in which he promised that proceeds from closing the smaller monasteries would be committed to good causes. As with so many promises from government, this one was never fulfilled and the proceeds finished up somewhere in the Treasury.

Although it was one of the larger monasteries, Romsey Abbey certainly contributed to their generally poor reputation for it had a long history of scandals. It hit a new low under Abbess Elizabeth Broke who in 1478 confessed to perjury and adultery amidst allegations of financial mismanagement (1). Under subsequent abbesses, the Abbey never seemed to recover from this event and early in 1539 it was surrendered to the King. It was a sad ending for a monastery that had once been renowned for its piety and good work.

Romsey parishioners buy the Abbey Church and Processional Way
During the rule of the abbesses, Romsey parishioners had been allowed to use the north aisle of the Abbey Church for worship. As the population increased, more space was needed and in the 1400s the Bishop of Winchester gave permission for parishioners to use the north transept and to build an extension to the north aisle. This newly formed area was known as the Church of St Laurence.

At the time of the Dissolution, there was no other church in Romsey so in1544 parishioners were allowed to buy the whole of the Abbey Church from the King. They paid £100 for it – a considerable sum of money at that time and the large church would subsequently prove to be a great burden on the small community that had to maintain it. The original conveyance, signed by Henry, is displayed in the south aisle of the Abbey. A translation of it made in 1774 by the Reverend Watson shows that in addition to the church, the sale also included a piece of land around it:
"... for an ambit and a processional way and not otherwise to be exercised and used containing in breadth twenty four feet by standard measure...".

It was the 24 ft wide Processional Way running along the west wall of the Abbey Church which caused Churchwardens Biggs and Clark such concern some 200 years later and it recurs throughout the story of Romsey's Public Walk and Pleasure Ground.

1.Henry Liveing – 'Records of Romsey Abbey' – an account of the Benedictine House of Nuns. (1912)

1773 – The Processional Way is lost but churchwarden Biggs rides to the rescue

The Abbey Church in the 18th century

By the early 1700s the area around the Abbey Church had changed significantly since the people of Romsey had bought the building from King Henry. On the churchyard side, the extension to the north aisle that had been built to make extra room for the congregation of St Laurence's Church had been demolished. It was no longer required now parishioners had use of all of the church. On the south side of the church, most of the domestic buildings used by the nuns had been pulled down.

The large bell tower of St Laurence's Church that once stood at the rear entrance to what is now the Magistrates' Court had become unsound and had been pulled down in 1625. Its six heavy bells had been removed to the tower of the Abbey Church that had been altered to accommodate them.

The Processional Way becomes blocked

During the incumbency of the Reverend John King (1728-1740) the Processional Way was still used for its intended purpose. There is a report (1) of a procession taking place around the church in which *"two old men went first, the vicar next, after him the clerk, then the sexton and the rest in order, that they met in the vestry, went out at the south door, turned to the right…"*. However, this procession seems to have been among the last of its kind.

Churchwardens had agreed that the vicar should have a garden to the east and the south sides of the church and to make it private and secure they built a wall around it with broken glass bottles cemented on the top to fend off raids by local children. The wall ran parallel to the sides of the church and around the south side as far as the south door. The vicar was an enthusiastic gardener and soon had the substantial plot under cultivation. But with an astonishing disregard for the fabric of the fine old building, he planted fruit trees close to the church and nailed their branches to its ancient stones.

Sketch of the west end of the church showing a door in the wall built by churchwardens (from a drawing by Dr Latham of about 1800)

A few years later, churchwardens built yet another wall which ran from the southwest corner of the church. This wall had a door in it that opened on to the Processional Way and was used by churchgoers as a short cut on their way home. At the time there was an open field reaching all the way from the west end of the church down to the River Test. An engraving made in 1777 is reproduced on the front cover of this book and gives an idea of how open the area may have looked, although the artist may have tidied up the scene to make it more attractive. The owners of the field used it for grazing their cattle but there was no clear boundary between the field and the Processional Way so the animals were free to roam right up to the church wall. About 10 years after the south-west wall had been built, owners of the field blocked up the doorway. Churchgoers and churchwardens were very put out.

In 1737, a meeting of churchwardens (a Vestry) resolved that the doorway should be reopened for the churchgoers. Following negotiations with owners of the land, it was agreed that churchwardens should pay them two shillings and six pence per annum for the right to cross it. Churchwardens paid the rent for the first few years but then they stopped; the owners did not press for payment and the matter became forgotten. However, churchwardens had not forgotten that the Processional Way was Church land and they subsequently made several unsuccessful attempts to recover it from their neighbours.

In 1773, the door was blocked up again. By then, the field immediately to the west of the church was no longer used for grazing cattle and had been turned into the garden of nearby Abbey House which was part of a large holding of land and property to the south and west of the church known as the Abbey Estate. The garden walls of Abbey House had been built so that they came right up to the church and blocked the Processional Way.

Churchwarden Biggs to the rescue

Despite the fact that the garden of Abbey House had reached up to the church walls for several years, one of the churchwardens, William Biggs, took great exception to the Processional Way being blocked. He complained to Josiah Merryweather who lived in Abbey House but Merryweather said he was only a tenant in the house and not the owner; Abbey Estate owned the house and where its garden walls went was not his problem. An argument broke out and the continuing animosity between the two men became well known in the town.

Another member of the Biggs' family, George, was also a churchwarden and it seemed that both William and George were men of action and had little patience with the measured and leisurely approach of the Vestry. George had recently incurred a large bill by repairing the church clock without authorisation from the churchwardens who were so annoyed that they recorded their complaint at the subsequent Vestry meeting adding *"and we will not pay"*.

News of William Biggs' dispute with Merryweather had reached William Daman, a noted solicitor with offices in his Church Street house. Daman was clearly aware of Biggs' awkward disposition and publicly warned him that if he got involved in legal action with Merryweather it would have to be at his own expense as the parish was not behind him.

Nevertheless, on a fine October day, and with Daman's warning still ringing in his ears, Biggs forced his way into Merryweather's garden, tore down the walls and shrubs and threw aside everything that was blocking the Processional Way. The path around the Church was now open once again.

Despite his reputation, Biggs' loutish behaviour surprised local people and caused a rift amongst churchwardens and amongst inhabitants of the town. One group felt that Biggs had been motivated more by pique against Merryweather than a genuine desire to recover church property and they would only support an amicable solution to the dispute. Another group, conscious of the fact that the Processional Way had been bought from the King, thought that the Church should try to recover it but they did not approve of Biggs' methods.

The Church seeks legal advice
At their next Vestry, churchwardens decided to seek legal advice on how the Processional Way might be recovered. In a large document titled "CASE" they laid out the history of the land from the time they had purchased it. They described the walls they had built in the early 1700s and everything that had happened through to the present date of September 1773 except Biggs' assault on Merryweather's garden that they evidently thought it prudent to omit. Under the heading 'QUERY' they asked how the land might be recovered and voiced other concerns such as how the law might regard the evidence of elderly witnesses who lived nearby and could remember back to when the Processional Way had been used for its intended purpose.

The Church's Counsel John Madocks replied from Lincolns Inn in the following month by writing on the same document under the heading 'OPINION' as was the custom at the time. He noted that the sale of the Church and the Processional Way had been made to churchwardens and inhabitants of the town who were thereby created a "body corporate" so they could be recognised as purchasers. However, the situation was complicated by the fact that tenants of the Abbey Estate such as Merryweather, being inhabitants of the town, were also members of the body corporate. There was also a problem with evidence from the elderly witnesses because they lived locally and might, therefore, be prejudiced. Nevertheless, Madocks argued that the best way forward would be to go to law and to start by giving all the facts about the case to the Attorney in Winchester.

Despite his failings, there is no doubt that Biggs must have been a convincing talker for during the next few months he persuaded the majority of the churchwardens, despite their reservations, to go along with Madocks' recommendation. In May 1774 a long letter outlining the Church's claim to the Processional Way was sent to Edward Thurlow, the Attorney in Winchester. This was quickly followed by a letter from the

Abbey Estate denying the Church's claim to the Processional Way and asking that it be dismissed. They argued that the Processional Way had been part of their estate for such a long time that the Church had lost any rights it may once have had. Additionally, they recalled that the Church had previously paid rent to them in order to use the land; this was surely an acknowledgement that it belonged to the Abbey Estate.

At the time, the churchyard (sometimes called the north Garth) was not rectangular as it is today because the northwest corner was owned by the Abbey Estate. This piece of land was of far more use to the Church as a churchyard than the western part of the Processional Way that was in dispute. Thus, the vicar, John Peveril (2), proposed that the Church give up its claim to the Processional Way in exchange for the piece of land which would make the churchyard rectangular. The Abbey Estate agreed this proposal but insisted, among other things, that the parish pay their legal costs *"as it was owing to the obstinacy and folly of one or two men of the parish that any prosecution was commenced at all"*.

The Church proceeds to Chancery

At a Vestry on 26th January 1775, this response was found to be unacceptable and the Vestry declared they did *"hereby consent and desire that the proceedings in Chancery be carried on with vigour and effort in the four names above"*. One of the four names was, of course, William Biggs who attached to the minutes a copy of an order he had made to lawyer Charles Knott authorising him to proceed with legal action. This was certainly an aggressive response from the churchwardens. Writing from London at the time, William Fletcher noted that it was extraordinary that the whole parish should suffer themselves to be governed by one or two people *"particularly to justify the honour of Biggs and company"*.

However, one of the churchwardens who had not supported Biggs' cause, James Jackman, met with 14 prominent local townspeople who jointly signed a document demanding that further negotiation with the Abbey Estate should take place before the Church proceeded to Chancery. Unless this took place, they would not contribute to the legal costs. This, together with some doubts about whether their claim would really be successful, completely unsettled the churchwardens who resolved once again to seek advice from their Counsel.

A surprising response from Counsel

Another 'CASE-QUERY-OPINION' document was prepared again detailing the whole situation and asking if churchwardens should proceed to Chancery or drop the matter at this stage. Three separately considered opinions were received. All were astonishingly different from the original advice given by Madocks although there had been no change in the situation. In the opinion of each and every Counsel, the parish was advised to drop the case.

In a final show of bravado, churchwardens wrote to the Abbey Estate spelling out their terms for settling the dispute and threatening to commence proceedings in Chancery if they were not accepted. However, Romsey was then much smaller than it is now; Counsel's advice to drop the case must have been well known about the town and the Abbey Estate did not take the threat seriously.

The parish had failed in its attempt to recover the Processional Way and had also lost the opportunity to obtain extra churchyard space which they desperately needed and which they had to purchase later on (3). Abbey House and the surrounding land passed through several hands before John Latham bought it in the 1790s. Subsequently, his bankruptcy set the scene for the next part of this story - the founding of Romsey's Public Walk and Pleasure Ground.

1. From Dr Latham's Notes on the History of Romsey p 225/152. Most of this chapter is taken from these notes.
2. John Peveril was the vicar of the Abbey Church from 1740 to 1780.
3. Hampshire Record Office ref: 10M58PW103/4/5

1826 – Romsey people buy a Public Walk and Pleasure Ground

Latham's bankruptcy leads to substantial sales of land

John Latham was the son of Romsey's local historian, Dr Latham, but clearly did not inherit his father's thoughtfulness and circumspection. Over a period of about 20 years, this ambitious but reckless businessman acquired a chain of local inns and property mostly connected with his brewing activity. However, the properties were all mortgaged and he solved financial problems as they occurred by arranging further loans including substantial sums from his father. In 1817 the debt-laden business collapsed and John Latham was declared bankrupt (1). As a result, a considerable amount of land and property to the south and the west of the Abbey Church came up for sale. Much of this was bought by Romsey Corporation and part of it was to become the town's Public Walk and Pleasure Ground.

Romsey's first Town Hall in the Market Place had housed the

This building was the Town Hall in the 1820s. It stood on the site of the present Church Hall

Corporation since the 17th century but as the Corporation grew, it gradually transferred its base to the Audit House that had been built in the middle of Market Place by the first Lord Palmerston. By 1820, the Audit House was in a dire state of repair and there was an urgent need for the Corporation to find themselves new premises. It was suggested that the old malthouse (built by John Latham on the site of the present church rooms) could be converted into a town hall at a reasonable cost. The Corporation resolved to purchase it and by the 9th November 1822 the malthouse and much of the surrounding land became theirs.

The Corporation were clearly shrewd operators and had thought carefully about how to make the purchase a financial success by selling off parts of the land they did not need. Their plans can be seen in the 1822 conveyances which they marked up to show three areas that they proposed to sell on to John Young, James Sharp and the Church. The piece of land to be sold to the Church was the 24ft wide strip on the west side of the Abbey Church, the Processional Way, which Churchwarden Biggs had fought to recover in the 1770s.

Lord Palmerston proposes the town should have a Public Walk and Pleasure Ground
At about this time, Lord Palmerston noted that the town had no public ground and proposed that the area to the west of the Abbey (now sold to Young and Sharp) be repurchased and turned into a Public Walk and Pleasure Ground. He offered to pay £100 towards the cost. The Corporation immediately responded to this proposal by appointing a committee to re-purchase the land by public subscription. To complete the purchase they needed to raise £541. Sir Thomas Heathcote, MP for Hampshire, was to head the committee and it s members included the Mayor (James Sharp), the Town Clerk (Henry Holmes).

At this time, the Corporation, the Church and Lord Palmerston (the largest ratepayer and landowner) held power in Romsey. These three worked closely together and between them were responsible for most things spiritual and temporal that took place in the town. It was in the interests of inhabitants to avoid conflict with this powerful triumvirate; thus Young and Sharp readily agreed to sell their newly acquired pieces of land back to the Corporation.

Expressed in the conveyances (2) dated the first and second days of December 1826 describing the repurchase of the pieces of land are the words that provide the legal basis for the Public Walk and Pleasure Ground. The Corporation was to hold the land:
"Upon Trust to permit the said pieces or parcels of ground to be used at all times for ever hereafter as a Public Walk or Pleasure Ground for all orderly and peaceable persons".

These words are clearly intended to create a Public Trust and such expression in conveyances is still recognised as binding by the present day Charity Commission.

The Church, however, did not participate in Lord Palmerston's scheme to form a Public Walk and Pleasure Ground. It had ideas of its own.

A new burial ground?
At about this time, churchwardens decided to seek legal advice from their Counsel on a number of issues.

Among the questions asked in this document was one concerning the degree of control that churchwardens could exert over the appearance of pews which parishioners had been 'customising' to suit themselves. Some of the pews had been removed and then returned decorated with screens and drapes, etc as the 'owners' fancied. The interior of the church was clearly beginning to look like a circus. Churchwardens wanted to know what they could legally do about it.

Another question related to burial charges. Churchwardens were restricted to charging no more than 10/6d for burials in the churchyard but surely they could charge much more than that if the burial was in other ground such as the land that lay to the west and south of the church?

It was clear that the Church did not plan to buy the 24 ft wide strip in order to return it to its original use as a Processional Way. They wanted to use it as a burial ground if they could charge more for burials there than in the churchyard.

Henry Holmes is outraged
News of this plan reached the Town Clerk, Henry Holmes. He was a much-respected solicitor and a Master Extra in Chancery; a high office in the Court of Chancery. He had been involved in all the purchases and repurchases of land concerning the Public Walk and Pleasure Ground as well as being a member of the fundraising committee. Consequently he felt passionately that gravestones should not be set in the Processional Way to spoil the view of the west end of the church across the Public Walk.

He expressed his outrage at the churchwardens' proposal in a public notice (3) addressed to all parishioners in May 1825.

In the notice, Holmes made the point that on best legal advice the Processional Way belonged to the parishioners and not to the Church. The churchwardens had no power over it except as trustees for the parishioners. Consequently it was for the parishioners to decide whether or not the land should be used as a burial ground. He urged them to reject the churchwardens' scheme and to support Lord Palmerston:

"...in his generous endeavour to promote the convenience of the inhabitants [of Romsey]*, and exhibit to advantage, a magnificent specimen of Gothic Architecture".*

Holmes was successful in his appeal and the Processional Way was not used for burials. He would not have been happy, however, to know that in the 21st century, a supposedly more enlightened age, we allow half of the Public Walk to be used as a car park. This diminishes the view of the west end of the church far more than a few gravestones near the wall of the church would ever have done.

Romsey gained its Public Walk and Pleasure Ground in 1826 and it was an immediate success. It was used for shows and fairs and was well tended by the Corporation. Mudies *Hampshire* (1840) describes it as *"... a spot of green tastefully laid out with shrubs and flowers, and along the green there flows one of the ramifications of the Test."*

Because of Holmes' background and his intense interest in the matter, it seems likely that he would have drawn up a full Deed of Trust for the Public Walk that would have defined its boundaries, its use and the Trustees. To date, only a part of such a document has been found; it specifies the obligations of the Trustees and is reproduced as an appendix to this book.

Did the Church ever buy the Processional Way?
When the Corporation bought land to the south and the west of the Abbey Church in 1822 it made clear how it would dispose of land that it did not want. The original deeds are marked up to show that pieces of land were

to be sold to James Sharp and John Young and the 24 ft strip adjacent to the Abbey Church was to be sold to the Church

As explained earlier, the Church's interest in buying this strip of land was to use it as a burial ground and, in fact, in a subsequent indenture the strip is marked *"Burying Ground"* whereas in 1822 it was described as *"Land to be sold to the Church"*. In subsequent deeds, the land is described as *"Church property"*. No deeds describing a conveyance of the 24ft strip from the Corporation to the Church have been found. This is remarkable if the Church really did buy the land as all other documents relating to this matter have been well preserved.

The intention to purchase the land was clear in the Vestry minutes of the time which state that following the purchase the deeds were to be framed and hung on the Vestry wall. However, it seems most likely that the churchwardens changed their minds about buying the land when they heard from Counsel that they would not be allowed to charge more to use it as a burial ground than elsewhere. On the 19th May 1825 the Vestry minutes noted: *"That the land at the west end of the Church belonging to the parish be used as a Public Walk in the daytime and not as a burying ground"*. (nb: at that time, the Public Walk was kept locked at night).

This seems to confirm that the churchwardens had abandoned their intention to buy the land and in fact, the subject is not mentioned in subsequent Vestry minutes. It appears to be fairly conclusive evidence that the Church never bought the land. The problem remains however that in many subsequent conveyances the strip is described as being the property of the Church. It is one of those things which will probably remain a mystery and it might just as well remain so.

1. 'The Latham Bankruptcy, 1817' nicely described by Barbara Burbridge in LTVAS publication POTS & PAPERS No6, Autumn 1994.
2. These conveyances are held by Test Valley Borough Council in Andover although copies will be available in HRO ref 179A07.
3. HRO ref 27M60/130/3

1855 – Avery Moore comes to town and builds a new vicarage

Lots of new vicarages in the 1800s
In ancient times, it was obligatory that a new church should have land known as glebe land to support its priest and, in fact, a new church could not be consecrated without it. Houses, known as glebe houses were built on this land for the priest to live in. During the monastic period, however, many of the clergy who served parishes were also monks, and as they lived in the monasteries, the glebe houses fell out of use. Immediately following the Dissolution, a shortage of houses for the clergy became apparent but it was not until 1777 that the Gilbert Act (1) was passed which allowed clergy to borrow up to two years of the net income of their benefice in order to build vicarages. The Act was later amended to allow borrowing of up to three times the annual income of the benefice and it resulted in many new vicarages being built over the ensuing hundred years or so.

1855 – a new vicar
In 1854, having served the Abbey Church for four years, Canon Walter Carus found a new position in Winchester and was replaced by his friend,

the Reverend Charles Avery Moore. From the moment he arrived in Romsey it was clear that building a large and impressive vicarage close to the Abbey Church was uppermost in his mind. The problems he encountered in achieving this ambition proved to be a challenge to the strength of the Public Trust which protected Romsey's Public Walk and Pleasure Ground. These problems were to be echoed in the 1980s when the present vicarage was built alongside that of Avery Moore.

The Reverend Charles Avery Moore

The dedication shown by the vicar to building a new vicarage was quite remarkable. Letters written to his friend Walter Carus show he had spent a huge amount of time studying potential sites and how they could be developed. The inclusion of such fine detail led to letters of inordinate length which, taken with his scratchy handwriting, made them distinctly heavy going. Walter must have been a very good friend indeed.

A site for the new vicarage

Clearly the most prestigious site for the new vicarage would have been on one of the corners made by the junction of Church Street and Church Place (formerly Abbey Approach). Here it would stand at the busy approach to the church and at the same time be close to important local dignitaries and trades people who lived and worked nearby. Avery Moore's first choice, the land now occupied by the Magistrates Court, proved to have too many difficulties and he turned his attention to the corner now occupied by the fish and chip shop at 12 Church Street. This time his plans went as far as commissioning a drawing (see opposite page) of the proposed new vicarage. It can be seen how grandiose a vision he had of his new house.

Benjamin Ferrey, an architect of quite some repute, had been commissioned to design the new vicarage. A Hampshire man, he had

The architect Benjamin Ferrey

studied under Pugin (the elder) and had set up a practice in London that quickly grew to a remarkable size. In 1855 he was 45 years old and had a number of buildings to his credit including All Saints Church in Dorchester and St Stephens in Westminster. He was destined to win the RIBA Gold Medal in 1870. Ferrey estimated the cost of the new vicarage to be £1,250 but in a letter to the Bishop of Winchester, Avery Moore scoffed at the figure saying it was *"far too high"*; at his last parish he had built a new vicarage for only £1,120.

News of Avery Moore's feverish activity reached the *Romsey Register* newspaper (a forerunner to the *Romsey Advertiser)*. Commenting on the prospect of a new vicarage in the town the newspaper noted: *"...the living is small - only £250 per annum after paying a Curate's stipend. There is no house attached to the church, and as no suitable one can be rented or purchased in the town, the vicar is obliged to reside at a distance of nearly two miles from the church"*. In the first of a series of coincidences, this justification for a vicarage in 1855 – that the vicar had a long journey to the church – was used successfully in 1986 when the present vicarage was built despite local opposition and planning inquiries.

The two sites chosen by Avery Moore on Church Street had been built up

for some hundreds of years and there were immense difficulties in persuading people to move out or to sell their properties to make way for a new vicarage. Despite all

Benjamin Ferrey's design for a vicarage to be sited at the corner of Church Street and Church Place

Avery Moore's efforts, these problems proved to be insuperable and he was forced to look for another site. A second-best location was to the west end of the church alongside the Public Walk on land which was owned by John Young (the same who had sold land to the Corporation in 1826). Here it was not necessary to demolish any buildings and a handsome new vicarage in that position would be seen by churchgoers as they made their way to the north entrance of the church. Young was persuaded to part with a piece of land immediately north of the Public Walk and early in 1855 the conveyance was completed. However, the southern boundary of the site adjoining the Public Walk was ragged and there was a small indentation (or "nook" as Avery Moore described it) biting into the plot. This was to cause the vicar a great deal of trouble.

Benjamin Ferrey was called in to redesign the building for the new site. The new vicarage was to have concrete foundations and was among the first in the area to have water closets. Romsey had no sewerage system until the 1930s so a cesspit 10ft deep had to be dug in the garden. A 40ft deep well would be required and water from it would be pumped up to a large tank in the roof to provide a constant supply. Marble fireplaces were to be fitted; Purbeck and Bath stone were specified to be used in the construction of the house. The wine cellar was given particular attention; it was to have two tiers of stone shelves with brick divisions and bottle racks fitted. It was beginning to sound really good; a very desirable residence suitable for a man of some importance. Ferrey estimated it would cost £1,500 to build.

Raising the cash

Most of the money was to come as a loan from the Church Authorities but donations of a hundred pounds each were expected from Lord Palmerston, Lady Palmerston and Mrs Noel (the wife of a former vicar the Reverend Gerard Noel). As Avery Moore himself observed, the benefice was quite small, producing only £327-7s-4d per annum and the most he would be allowed to borrow was £1,250.

At this time, the Abbey Church was badly in need of repairs to the gutters and parapets and a plan to rebuild the nave roof, a very costly undertaking, had been under discussion for several years. Once again, Ferrey was called in to estimate the cost of putting the church to rights. This came to £2,300 and churchwardens decided to borrow the money from the Loans Society. In view of this, it would not seem to have been a good time for Avery Moore to be thinking about an expensive new vicarage but in listing potential sources of funding in one of his many letters he simply notes that the parish could not help him *"as they have to pay for the repairs of the church"*.

He decided that he would make up the shortfall in the cash he needed by public subscription.

A problem with the site

The first sign of a problem with the location of the new vicarage came in a letter (2) dated 18th May 1855 from Avery Moore to the Corporation asking if he could lease the Public Walk adjacent to his building plot and turn it into a garden. A few days later, he wrote to the Mayor saying that he had discussed his plans to lease the Public Walk with Lord Palmerston and he had been authorised to say that his Lordship *"most fully approves the land being vested in the vicar provided that there is no building upon it"*. It is a mark of the times that Lord Palmerston, who had been elected Prime Minister only three months earlier and was faced with a serious problem in the Crimea where the war was going badly, had found time to become fully acquainted with Avery Moore's little problem and was prepared to become involved in it. Palmerston was not a particularly religious man. Somewhat caustically, Lord Salisbury once remarked of him that the only vicar he ever spoke to was the vicar of Romsey(3).

Avery Moore asked for a reply from the Corporation as soon as possible

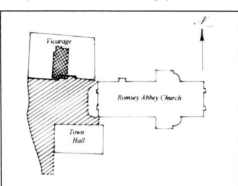

This sketch shows the overlap between the vicarage (double hatched) and the Public Walk (hatched). The Town Hall was then on the site of the present Church Hall.

"as it will determine the position of my house". The difficulty was that the house as planned with its outhouses to the north was too big to fit in the centre of his building plot because the "nook" in the boundary overlapped the foundation of the house. There was room to put the house at the back of the plot but then there would have been no space for the elaborate ornamental garden he was planning.

The mayor, Dr Francis Taylor, wrote to say that the Corporation would not entertain the idea of giving up the Public Walk to the vicarage. However, an alternative proposal that there could be an exchange of land, was something they would approve *"provided the Corporation had the legal right to do so"*. Encouraged by this, Avery Moore offered £5 for the small area he needed. The Corporation again agreed subject to *"agreement from the Treasury"*. In 1855 the Municipal Corporations Acts (which governed procedures of town Corporations) required that they sought approval from external organisations for their actions in certain matters. In the case of the Public Walk, where the land was subject to a Public Trust, the Inclosure Office and the Lords

Commissioners of Her Majesty's Treasury (the Treasury for short) were the appropriate authorities.

By July 1855, Avery Moore had sensed there was going to be a problem with the Treasury and that things were not going to turn out as he had planned. He persuaded the Corporation to agree to give him the piece of land and wrote to the Church Commissioners asking them to arrange a conveyance. He said he did not want the title of the land to be investigated as there was nothing wrong with it – he was merely trying to save costs!

However, the Church Commissioners didn't fall for that. They wrote seeking advice from their Counsel Charles Ker – a man of some standing who was also the Recorder of Andover and Conveyancing Counsel to the Reformed Court of Chancery. Ker's view was uncompromising: because of the Public Trust regulating the land, the Corporation had no power to *"alienate"* it. That is to say, the Corporation could neither exchange, sell nor even give it away.

In matters such as this, Charles Ker was the ultimate authority and most men would surely have accepted his judgement and revised their plans.

The vicar, however, was not as most men.

The foundation stone is laid and building begins
Avery Moore was now under some pressure. If the new vicarage was not completed early in the following year, he would have to pay another £60 to extend the lease on the house at Abbotswood where he was living. Determined to have his vicarage in the centre of the plot, he decided to commence building despite the fact that his efforts to resolve the boundary problem with the Corporation, the Church Commissioners and the Treasury had come to nothing. He arranged for a ceremony to take place on 11th September 1855 when the foundation stone of the new vicarage would be laid.

The ceremony was a splendid occasion. It was held on the Public Walk and Pleasure Ground and attended by the vicar and his family, the mayor, aldermen, many local dignitaries, the church choir and over 600 school children from local schools together with their 40 teachers. It began

Avery Moore's grand new vicarage completed in 1856 (photo circa 1910)

promptly at 1 o'clock with a peal of bells which was followed by an alarmingly lengthy address from the vicar who among many other things, expressed his thanks to everyone who had contributed to the £650 which had been raised by the public subscription committee. The *Romsey Register* covered the ceremony in great detail regretting that space did not permit reproduction of the whole of the vicar's address. However, the long and laborious excerpt they did print showed that the whole speech must have been quite numbing for the 600 children present. After the address, the foundation stone was laid by Mrs Susan Noel and an hermetically sealed vessel containing an article on the ceremony together with a coin of the Realm was placed in the foundations.

Following the ceremony, the children were taken by two wagons to Whitenap Park where they enjoyed games, tea and buns until 8pm when they were brought back to the Public Walk to sing the national anthem. Then they were dismissed by the vicar, rounding off a day, said the *Romsey Register "which they will never forget"*.

This day was a truly remarkable celebration of the founding of the new vicarage considering the vicar was about to build it in the wrong place!

Picking up his boundary problem again, Avery Moore wrote to the Treasury and to Lord Palmerston to seek their support for the transfer of the piece of land he now desperately needed. The Treasury, after all, had not actually said that such a transfer was impossible and they might still be persuaded to agree, especially since part of the foundation of the vicarage was now laid on the Public Walk. Lord Palmerston readily gave his support but the response from the Treasury was distinctly frosty.

Writing on the 20th November 1855, John Greenwood, the assistant solicitor to the Treasury wrote: *"In this rule of things, you ask me to have the Treasury and the Commissioners parties to the conveyance. If you forgive me, I think you can hardly have reflected on what you ask... What Officer of their Lordships would advise them to concur in a Grant which creates a breach of trust upon its face?"*.

The vicar's anxiety increases and all patience is exhausted

By now, building work on the new vicarage was well advanced and Avery Moore began to get very anxious, as there seemed no way for him to get possession of the piece of the Public Walk on which his house was built.

Some measure of his desperation can be found in this heavily underscored extract from a letter he wrote to Lord Palmerston at the time: *"...the blame must rest upon me, not the architect, for placing the south wall upon the ground in question! I held back until I had obtained the formal pledge of the Mayor of the Corporation handed to me in writing with the official seal attached! - the formal approval of the Treasury announced by letter and the formal consent of the Church Commissioners to accept the conveyance...".*
In a letter to the mayor, Lord Palmerston pointed out that what the vicar was saying was not true; he had not waited for the formal approval of any of these bodies.

Apparently insensitive to the tenor of the advice he had received from the Treasury, in his anxiety he wrote to them yet again making excuses for his actions and asking them to reconsider their reply.

During January and February 1856, his ceaseless efforts to resolve the problem wore everybody down. The Treasury made a very dismissive response to his request for them to think again and the Inclosure Office wrote making absolutely clear the Corporation's legal situation regarding the Trust. His solicitor, Tylee, was clearly miffed as he returned all the letters concerning the vicarage to Avery Moore with a letter which began *"I didn't like the letter you sent me....".* In the Corporation, Town Clerk Harry Porter Curtis was deeply offended. He discovered that what he had thought had been a confidential discussion with the vicar concerning the possible support and involvement of Lord Palmerston had been made public in Avery Moore's letters. These had apparently turned a helpful suggestion into a presumption. Lord Palmerston himself had every right

Deeply offended – Town Clerk Harry Porter Curtis

to be offended and it now seemed that the vicar was all alone with his problem and the goodwill and patience of all the people he had involved was completely exhausted.

The resolution

Avery Moore then decided to resolve the problem in his own way. He built a stone wall to the south of the vicarage just as it stands today. It encompassed the troublesome 'nook' and another slice of the Public Walk so that the boundary was now a straight line. And, one has to say, it looks quite well and nobody has ever complained.

Early in 1857, Benjamin Ferrey personally inspected both the house and the bills submitted by the builder, George Wheeler, and found them to be satisfactory. £1,787-2s-6d was payable for the house and £153-4s-5d for the fences and gates bringing the total to £1,940-6s-11d. Of this sum, £1,250 had come as a loan from the Queen Anne's Bounty and the remaining £690-6s-11d as cash from the vicar which he had raised by public subscription.

By strange chance, the last letter found on this subject is from the Inclosure Office to Avery Moore seeking details of his problem. They wanted to know all about it because it was just the kind of case they could take to Parliament in order to bring about a change in the law. The amendment they proposed would have allowed Avery Moore and the Corporation to agree the sale or exchange of the small piece of land which had caused so much trouble. The Inclosure Office had previously written to his lawyer, Mr Tylee, but much to their astonishment he appeared to have completely forgotten everything about it. Could Avery Moore please help them? The vicar must have winced when he read the letter. But there are times when it is prudent to say nothing and to do nothing. This was certainly one of them. And that is just what he did – nothing.

Romsey Abbey Church, Hants.

The Public Trust survives
All this fuss had been about a tiny piece of land only a few square yards in area. Despite this and despite the fact that Lord Palmerston and the Corporation had bent over backwards to assist the vicar, the Public Trust governing the Public Walk and Pleasure Ground had proved to be resilient. The challenge to the Trust had been referred to the highest level in the country, to the Lords Commissioners of Her Majesty's Treasury, the Inclosure Office and the Church Commissioners who had all agreed that the Trust could not be 'alienated'.

As we shall see, the passing of time weakened the resolve of the Trustees (the Corporation and its successors) properly to administer the Trust. It was not until around the year 2000 that a serious effort was made to have the Trust acknowledged.

Avery Moore's problems were not yet over. Among an array of letters about his dispute with his neighbours at Abbey Mills, trouble over the Church Rate and tireless attempts to get his stipend increased, it is astonishing to find he had the nerve to test the strength of the Public Trust once again as described in the following chapter.

1. This paragraph is based on chapter II of JH Blunt's 'Book of Church Law' published in 1901
2. This letter and many others concerning the building of the vicarage can be found in the Hampshire Record Office ref: 10M58/PW118.
3. 'Lord Palmerston' by Jasper Ridley. Panther Books 1972.

1857 – Avery Moore has a problem with his horse and carriage

The vicar extends his glebe
When it was completed, the grand new house and its elaborately laid out gardens had all the appurtenances of a substantial and prosperous vicarage as befitted the magnificence of the Abbey Church. A visitor standing in the decorated porch would hear the sound of the doorknocker echo around the spacious rooms. Here was a house that had been built for a man of importance, a house which demanded deference to its owner.

However, large vicarages usually have large grounds or glebes attached to them and Avery Moore set about repairing this omission in his vicarage. His offer to convert the Public Walk and Pleasure Ground into a garden to be maintained by the Church had already been rejected by the Corporation so he turned his attention to the land behind the vicarage that was owned by Lord Palmerston. In April 1857 he acquired part of it in exchange for a meadow called 'Matins' that was owned by the Church. A few months later, he persuaded the Church Authorities to buy the remainder of it from Lord Palmerston. The vicarage now had a most impressive glebe stretching from the vicarage all the way down to the river Test, and from Mill Lane through to Abbey Meads.

Access across the Public Walk
But now there was a new problem. In a corner of the vicar's newly acquired land there was a coach house which he dearly wanted to use - for what could complement the picture of his vicarage more perfectly than a horse and carriage at the front door? The difficulty was that the shortest route from the coach-house to his front door was across the Public Walk. Bearing in mind that his house was unlawfully built on the Public Walk, it might have seemed prudent at this point not to press the issue of access across the land. But that was not Avery Moore's way. In March 1859 we find him writing (1) to the mayor complaining how unreasonable it was that to get from his coach-house to the front of the vicarage he was obliged to travel via Market Place, Church Street and Industry Road (Mill Lane). With remarkable audacity he offered the Corporation a yearly rent of one shilling to allow him access.

Perhaps because of his fondness for the vicar or as likely because of concern for the future of his soul, the mayor, Mr Beddome, replied that if it was his decision alone, he would give the good vicar *"carte blanche"*. However, he had a duty to refer the question to the Council. Things did not go quite as planned at the subsequent Council meeting because the mayor subsequently wrote to say that the question would have to be referred to another committee of which he was chairman but *"if my neighbour gets his way, you will have to pay five shillings per year!"*.

Considering all that had gone before, the Corporation resolved this problem by a remarkable fudge. On the 24th of May 1859, the Town Clerk, Harry Porter Curtis, wrote to say that the Corporation had, *"so far as they lawfully could"*, acceded to Avery Moore's request for access at a rent of one shilling a year on condition that he agreed that the Corporation could withdraw its consent at any time without notice. Or to put it another way; the Corporation could not lawfully grant access to the land but they were prepared to do so unlawfully for a shilling a year provided Avery Moore agreed to relinquish his rights at the drop of a hat if the Corporation got found out!

As chance would have it, the present day trustees, the Borough Council (TVBC), found themselves confronted with the same access problem in 1985 when the new vicarage was planned and access to it would be required across the Public Walk. History then repeated itself to the letter. Maybe TVBC could have taken the same line as the Corporation but in fact they chose an entirely different approach as will emerge later.

In 1860 Avery Moore and his family moved to Sutterton (near Boston) to occupy a huge vicarage that had been built in 1724 by wealthy patrons of the 'Church of St Mary with Fosdyke'. It was pulled down in 1954 but the present vicar remembers it as *"twenty large rooms above cellars"*. His new glebe in Lincolnshire was an impressive 495 acres; vast compared with the few wretched acres he had fought to acquire in Romsey. Furthermore, his income had leapt from £455 to £1,032 as a result of his move. Perhaps he found some peace there.

1. HRO ref: 10M58/PW123

1875 – Berthon's encounters with the Public Walk

The Reverend Berthon and the Abbey Church

By the early 1800s the Abbey Church was in a sorry state. So many layers of whitewash had been applied to its interior since the practice first began in the 1600s that it had acquired the name *'the chalk pit'*. Many of the arches had been bricked up to keep out draughts, high wooden galleries had been built which, whilst they gave the congregation a better view of proceedings, diminished the spaciousness of the fine old building and did nothing to enhance the interior.

Between them, the Reverend Gerard Noel vicar from 1841 to 1849) and the Reverend Edward Berthon (1860 to 1892) did most of the work to

The Reverend Berthon

restore the building to the condition we see it in today. Berthon, in particular, was an imaginative engineer who brought his boat-building skills (1) to bear upon the difficult problems encountered in renovating such a large structure and probably saved the Church a great deal of money by his ingenuity.

There is no doubt that given more time and money, he would have achieved even more significant improvements to the church. For example, at a Vestry meeting in April 1877, churchwardens had raised the possibility of selling a piece of land known as *'the old belfry ground'*. This was a piece of land at the rear entrance to the present Magistrates Court where the belltower of St Lawrence's had once stood. In 1624 the bells were moved to the Abbey and the belltower was demolished in the following year. Since then, the Church had let the land. The suggestion of selling it was immediately dismissed by Berthon who said that the Church needed to retain it *"as it may one day be needed as a site on which to build a new belltower"*.

It emerged later that Berthon did not like the octagonal wooden structure which had been built on top of the church tower to accommodate the bells and he thought that lowering the ceiling of the church tower to house the bell-ringers had spoiled the interior of the Church. He was prepared to contemplate building a new belltower in order to be able to restore the Abbey Church to its former condition. In the event, the *'old belfry ground'* remained in possession of the Church until 1941 when it was bought by *'Gunner'* Moody (of the gunshop in Church Street) so that he and his sister could park their cars in the shed that had been built on it.

Lack of money certainly limited the execution of many of Berthon's ideas. At a Vestry meeting in April 1869, the shortage of cash was such that he ordered there was to be no unauthorised expenditure on the church, that the old custom of chiming would have to cease and the church clock would be stopped, in order to save money. From now on, Berthon declared, he would fund the church lighting from his own account so that services in the evening could continue without interruption. Furthermore, he would continue to do so until the churchwardens had found *"the necessary means"*, which, happily, they managed to do by the following year.

A small access problem
When Berthon moved into the vicarage in 1860, the wide gate that Avery Moore had erected to allow him to get his horse and carriage through to the road was still in place. Having no use for the gate, Berthon planted a holly hedge backed by a dense row of laurels which completely blocked it. However, fifteen years later, when the hedge had become a thick shrubbery, he cut a small way through to the Public Walk.

Within a matter of days he got a bill from the Corporation for one shilling payable as rent! Berthon cheerfully paid up but was asked to write a letter agreeing to the same terms as Avery Moore; that is, the Corporation would allow access (as far as they legally could) and that the agreement would be immediately revoked should anyone complain.

Berthon would like part of the Public Walk
Berthon was interested in improving the grand new vicarage he had inherited from Avery Moore. Perhaps as an ornament or possibly with

conservation in mind, he reassembled an arched stone window frame (left over from his work on the Abbey Church) in the rear garden of the vicarage where it makes a very attractive feature. The house later derived the name *Folly House* from this structure. Berthon would certainly have

The Folly House window frame

been aware of Avery Moore's problem with the site and his attempts to acquire the adjoining public land as part of the church glebe. Twenty years after the departure of Avery Moore, he thought it prudent to re-open the subject with the Corporation and this appears to have met with some success. In 1880 an agreement was drawn up between Berthon and the Corporation. It allowed Berthon to lease the triangle of land adjoining the vicarage (the area that is now grassed) provided he erected and maintained a fence around it. Surprisingly, the lease carried no caveat that Berthon should immediately give up his rights at the demand of the Corporation. Over the 25 years since Avery Moore's vicarage problem, the Corporation seemed to have become less diligent in its approach to the Public Trust that governed the use of the Public Walk.

For some reason that is not clear, Berthon suddenly dropped the idea. Possibly he had referred the lease to the Church Commissioners whose legal adviser, Mr Ker, had in 1855 so emphatically denied that the Corporation was legally entitled to let, sell or give away the land. However, in Berthon's time the Corporation had made up its mind to fence off and let the land. In doing so it breached the Public Trust.

Berthon's long and productive incumbency came to an end in 1892 when he was replaced by the Reverend Cooke Yarborough.

1. Berthon was remarkably inventive and among his inventions was a folding boat which was manufactured in Romsey on a site that is now Lortemore car park. A copy of his autobiography can be found in Romsey public library. See also LTVAS publication (2004) 'Rev E L Berthon' and the Vestry Minutes.

1895 – Cooke Yarborough's concern

The vicar's offer is declined

In 1895 there was yet another attempt by the Church to gain control of the Public Walk. The Reverend James Cooke Yarborough was vicar at the time and in a letter to the mayor he observed that the Public Walk, previously well maintained with flowerbeds and paths, had fallen into neglect and had become unsightly. Furthermore, he noted that the Corporation had railed off and let part of the land which was not the purpose for which it was intended. The vicar proposed (1) the Church should lay out the Public Walk as a garden and be responsible for its maintenance thus relieving the Corporation of the financial burden.

The Reverend Cooke Yarborough

In this proposal he was closely following one of Avery Moore's many ideas. Accompanying his letter to the Mayor was the same drawing that of the Public Walk that Avery Moore had sent to the Corporation when he was trying to gain control of the land. The drawing showed flowerbeds at each corner and one at the centre of the area.

Forty years had elapsed since Avery Moore had made his claim to the Public Walk and it is interesting to observe how often in this story the Church demonstrates a continuity of purpose and ideas (as perhaps one should expect of it). Only exceptionally, such as when the Corporation billed Berthon for using a gate after a lapse of some 20 years, is the Corporation capable of sustaining a comparable memory span. In a similar context, Henry Holmes observed in his notice to parishioners that the Church had lost the Processional Way *"through 'laches' or neglect; notwithstanding the maxim of law, that no Time runs against the Church"*

Cooke Yarborough's proposal to take over the Public Walk and the associated maintenance costs was turned down flat by the Corporation.

Quite possibly the phrase that the vicar had used in his letter: '[the Corporation] *has let and railed off part of the land which was not the purpose for which it was intended"* – had alerted the Corporation to the existence of the Public Trust. The Corporation not only refused to entertain Cooke Yarborough's idea but also ceased to let the land and had the railings removed.

An offer made with the best of intentions
Cooke Yarborough then gave notice that he intended to rail off *"that part of the land which does belong to the Church"* which was the Processional Way along the west wall of the Abbey. The railings remained there until the Second World War when they were removed together with those around the churchyard as scrap metal to assist in the war effort.

Some three years later, Cooke Yarborough seemed to feel it necessary to explain the reason behind his proposal to take over the Public Walk. In a letter to Henry Guard who was Romsey's town mayor at the time, he regretted the fact that the Corporation had not accepted his idea. He went on to explain that his intention was not to lay out the ground as a Public Walk and Pleasure Ground but rather to lay it to grass leaving a roadway: *"to show up the Abbey in which every inhabitant of Romsey takes a pride"*

The Reverend Cooke Yarborough's incumbency came to an end in 1910 – the year when the Church seized another opportunity to lay claim to the land.

1. HRO ref: 97M81/13/14

1910 – Another Church claim to Trust land

The 1910 Finance Act

This Act provided for a new tax on the *increase* in value of land over time. To make this possible, the value of all land in the United Kingdom as at 30th April 1909 had to be agreed. This was an enormous task in which the land was valued by valuation officers according to a complex set of rules. Provision was made for the landowners to appeal against valuation decisions and the overall administrative burden must have been immense. Together with continued opposition from landowners this contributed to the repeal of the Act in 1920.

However, records (1) of this work, much of which has survived, is of considerable value to local historians because they created a wealth of information known at the time as Lloyd George's Domesday Survey. The records are frequently in use today, mainly as evidence of rights of way when courts are required to determine right of access although they are of limited value for that purpose. This is because landowners were allowed a reduction in tax if there was a public right of way across their land. So some landowners who resented public intrusion on their property would fail to declare a footpath and others, who were keen to see a reduction in tax, would use their imagination to make sure a footpath was recognised.

The Church makes a another claim to the Trust land

In 1910, the Reverend Cooke Yarborough resigned his incumbency at Romsey Abbey Church and was replaced by Hugh Martin St Clair Timmer. At around this time, land valuation records show that the Church had claimed ownership of the triangular grassed patch between the old and the new vicarages which was of course part of the Trust land owned by the Council. The Church and the graveyard carry the allotment number 1346 and the triangular grassed area carries the same number. There is no supporting evidence for this claim: transactions between the Church and public bodies are normally well documented with references to be found in Vestry minutes, Corporation or council minutes and financial records of both parties. But no such evidence has been found showing that such a conveyance took place and this was later admitted by the Church in the Chancery case in October 2007.

The Church has always been very sensitive about its property and events such as that described in this book where it lost its right to the 24 ft wide strip around the church as a result of neglect are very rare. In this case though, it would seem that the council had been negligent in not taking up the matter with the Church and challenging their claim.

The church authorities would also have been alive to any change in legislation that would affect their land so it seems likely that the Reverend Cooke Yarborough and other vicars would have been asked to assess their situations during discussions and consultations which took place prior to the Finance Act being passed. As Cook Yarborough had expressed more than a passing interest in the Public Walk and Pleasure Ground, the claim would seem most likely to have originated from him.

Curiously, or perhaps understandably, the Church laid no claim to a piece of land they really did own; the "Old Belfry Ground" – the site of the Belfry taken down in the 1600s and rented out regularly until 1945 when they sold it to Moody (of Moody's gunshop in Church Street). There is no mention of it in the records. Not a trace.

Following the First World War, the Memorial Park was established and this took over the function of the Public Walk. With the growth in car ownership, part of the land was covered with tarmac so that it could be used as a car park.

1. HRO ref: 152M82 Land Valuation Books and BL catalogue ref: IR/125/4/645.

1985 – Another new vicarage but an old access problem

Some unpopular plans

In June 1984 the Diocese announced plans to sell the old vicarage built by Avery Moore in 1855 and to build a new one in its grounds. The plans showed that the new vicarage was to be built on the western boundary of the Public Walk. To reach the road, access would be required across it. Two designs, described as 'A' and 'B', were submitted for planning approval (1) where they met with considerable local opposition. There were objections to the style of the designs and to the desirability of building anything at all on that particular site at the heart of the town's conservation area. Planning permission was refused for both designs.

The Church Authorities appealed against this decision and, at the same time, submitted two further designs 'C' and 'D'. Local people, the Romsey and District Society and Test Valley Borough Council (the Planning Authority following local government reorganisation in 1974) objected to the schemes on the grounds of their appearance and their impact on the surroundings. In July 1985 these designs were also refused.

The Church then mounted another appeal and the subsequent inquiry began in February 1986. It lasted for two days during which the secretary of the Diocese of Winchester Diocesan Parsonages made the point, which became important in the final decision made on this application, that the Church could not operate efficiently unless the vicar lived close by. It will be remembered that the Reverend Avery Moore had also expressed the need to live near the church when justifying the building of his new vicarage in 1855. At the time, he was living in Abbotswood, some two miles from the church.

The result of the appeal came in a letter dated 22nd May 1986 from the Department of Environment and the Department of Transport. They had decided to accept schemes 'C' and 'D' and, in doing so, made the following notes:
In section (9):

"the council was not entirely satisfied that the whole of the triangular space was in the ownership or control of the appellant [the Church]*"*
(The "triangular space" being the grassed area of the Public Walk)
And in section (14):
"the penetration of vehicles across the triangular space is not in the interests of conservation".
It had been previously noted on page 3 para 2 that:
"...on the advice of the Historic Buildings Council, the Secretary of State for the Environment has accepted that the Romsey conservation area is outstanding".
The government departments had taken note of the points made by local

The new vicarage built in the 1980s

people, TVBC and the Romsey and District Society that this was indeed a very sensitive part of the conservation area.

The *Romsey Advertiser* noted that permission for schemes 'C' and 'D' was granted on the exceptional grounds that the new vicarage was needed so that the vicar could be close to the church.
Permission to build the new vicarage was granted nearly two years after the first application had been made.

Local views - the church rooms controversy revisited
A clue as to why it had taken so long to agree planning permission for the new vicarage lies in a letter to the *Romsey Advertiser* from a local resident. She noted with some surprise that the planning consultant for the Church Commissioners had said that they were striving for *"...a building that would fit in with the surrounding buildings including the modern ones; in particular the church rooms and the Magistrates Court".* Clearly, the writer did not think that the church rooms provided a good example for the design of the new vicarage. Another writer to the *Romsey Advertiser* recalled that many local people regretted the demolition of the old town hall to make way for the controversial design of the new church rooms and verger's house in 1966.

This was a sorry tale. Apparently aware of the sensitivity of the site, Hampshire County Council (HCC), the Planning Authority at the time,

Church Hall and Vergers house built in the 1960s

had referred the planning application for the church rooms to the Royal Institute of British Architects who, in turn, appointed a special panel of architects to consider it. In his report to HCC, the chairman of the panel wrote:

"The unique importance of this site merits a building of the highest quality. This should be referred to the County Panel and/or the Royal Fine Arts Commission. This design is completely unsympathetic with the

Ceremony at the site of the new Church Hall c1966

surroundings." The County Planning Officer who received the report wrote to the Area Planning Officer noting this comment but saying that he thought the *"mass"* of the building was satisfactory. He also thought that the north and west

elevations *"should be more in the ecclesiastical idiom"* and went on to suggest some minor changes to the exterior of the design. However, in another letter written some two weeks later he wrote that he had put the matter before the Council Panel. They did not feel that the case merited further reference either to the Town Planning Committee of the Hampshire and Isle of Wight Architectural Association or to the Royal Fine Arts Commission. They also thought it unwise to give the building an ecclesiastical character.

With a number of minor changes, permission was given to demolish the old town hall, jail and jail yard and to replace it with what we have today.

Subsequently, and after the church rooms had been built, a local architect sought planning permission to put a pitched roof on the rooms that, together with other modifications, would have resulted in a building that looked attractive and would have sat comfortably alongside the old vicarage and Abbey Church. But Hampshire County Council refused to give it planning permission.

The problem of access to the new vicarage

In reaching their decision to grant planning permission for the new vicarage, the government departments had left TVBC to sort out the difficult problem of access. This was exactly the same problem that

View across Public Walk along the vicarage drive to the Abbey Church (2004)

Avery Moore encountered in 1857 after he had acquired land behind his vicarage and wanted to drive his horse and carriage across the Public Walk. It will be remembered that the Corporation had fudged the issue by allowing Avery Moore access *"in so far as they legally could"* for a fee of one shilling per year.

So how, in 1986, would TVBC tackle the same problem?

Reporting on a TVBC Policy and Resources Committee held on 31st December 1986, the *Romsey Advertiser* recorded that following the meeting held to sort out the access problem, a Council official had said there was some doubt about the ownership of the land and that some of the conveyancing went back more than 100 years. The Church had been prepared to accept that the Council owned the land if the Council would allow access. Church and State would get together to try and resolve the problem.

A report in the *Southern Evening Echo* (headed: "Vicarage Row; Peace Nearer") notes that the Council's Policy and Resources Committee had met in secret. Prior to the meeting, it noted, both the Church and the Council had claimed ownership of the triangular green next to the existing vicarage over which access would have to be created.

These newspaper reports were greeted with some astonishment in the letters column of the *Romsey Advertiser* in the following week. One writer reminded readers that the Church had had to appeal against TVBC's refusal to give permission for the new vicarage but now the Council appeared to be doing all it could to make it possible. *"What has happened?"* she asked. Another reader wondered: *"... what is the collusion between Church and State?"*

Access problem seemingly resolved – but not for one shilling per annum
Perhaps it is because negotiations between the Church and the council were carried out in secret that it is so difficult to piece together the reasoning which finally allowed access to the vicarage across the Public Walk. And it is harder still, since nothing has apparently changed, to understand why it was possible to grant access in 1986 but not possible when Avery Moore had requested it in 1857.

Nonetheless, as the driveway to the vicarage has been regularly in use since the new building was erected, the access problem had, seemingly, been resolved. Some method of circumventing a requirement of the Trust that the land should not be alienated had apparently been found despite the clear requirement in the Trust that the land should not be alienated. Surely, there had not been another fudge like the one in 1857?

Sadly, in this case Test Valley Borough Council went far beyond a simple fudge. In exchange for an agreement that the Church would no longer claim ownership of the triangular grassed area, the council sold a small piece of the Trust land to the Church for £5,000 and access to the new vicarage was granted. This was a council selling charity land that it did not own! Furthermore, how the sale of a small piece of land permitted access across much more charity land is not easy to understand.

The access granted was just what Avery Moore had wanted in 1856 after he had built part of his house on Trust land. The vicar and Romsey Corporation had appealed to the highest authorities in the land and had been told that such a sale was forbidden as it would "alienate the trust". So it is extremely hard to understand how this deal could have been concluded legally.

In fairness to TVBC, it should be said that some 20 years later selling the land was recognized as a mistake and it was corrected.

Another surprising event at this time was that solicitors acting for the Church made use of a legal process to lay claim to part of the Public Walk. This was the triangular grassed area bounded by the two vicarages and The Abbey (road). In this process, a Statutory Declaration is made by a person who believes he, or the body he represents, is the true owner of a disputed or neglected piece of land. In time, provided this is not challenged, the claimant can become the legal owner.

Accompanying the Declaration was a four-page document in which the Church's solicitors reviewed a number of conveyances written between 1822 and 1856 and inferred that a transfer of land to the Church of some sort must have taken place although no conveyance was available to confirm that view. However, TVBC were aware of this claim and objected to it. The Church is not shown as the owner of this area on the Land Registry Index.

To make things more complicated HCC had at some time adopted The Abbey (road) that cuts across the Public Walk to Church Lane. It is not unusual in this situation for the County Council to adopt a verge at the side of the road but in this case, according to their records, they had adopted the whole of the triangular grassed area claimed by the Church. Hence, the grassed area, complete with oak tree and park bench, was considered officially to be highway land!

Local authorities as trustees
The Charity Commission has some clear views on this subject. One

advantage, they say, is that local authorities enjoy a perpetual succession so it is not necessary to make individual appointments of charity trustees. Another is that the authority may be willing to subsidise the charity out of its own funds or to provide professional services free of charge.

In the long experience of the Charity Commission, however, a major disadvantage is that they "often fail to appreciate that they are not free to deal with the property of a charity in the same way as they can deal with their own corporate property". This was certainly true of TVBC when it sold a piece of charity land to the Church in 1986. The Charity Commission also notes that politics may play a part in decisions made about the trust. As it turned out this is another observation that is very relevant to the Public Walk as can be seen in the following chapters.

1. Copies of letters and documents relating to the building of the new vicarage are held on microfiche at the TVBC Planning Office in Duttons Road, Romsey.

Events around the Millennium

The Public Walk revisited

In the 1990s, a local historian (who prefers to remain anonymous) came across references to the Public Walk and Pleasure Ground and transcribed

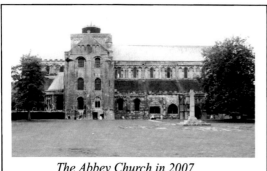

The Abbey Church in 2007

a number of letters and indentures from the 19th century that related to it. These indicated that the open ground to the west of the Abbey had at some time been placed in trust for the benefit of the inhabitants of Romsey. He had discussed the subject with senior TVBC officers and had arranged a meeting to take place in March 1999 between the Romsey's Town Clerk, Mayor, deputy Mayor and a representative from TVBC's legal department. At this time he asked the writer to take his place and pursue the matter.

The meeting proved to be a turning point in this story. The TVBC representative was familiar with much of the documentation concerning the building of the old vicarage in 1855 and the new one in 1986. It emerged that the originals of the 1826 indentures, in which Romsey Corporation repurchased the land it had sold to Young and Sharp (page 12) , were held by the Council in Andover. These indentures are critical as they are the only documents that have legal effect on the Trust governing the Public Walk and Pleasure Ground.

The situation at that time (1999) looked very confusing. Only parts of the open ground appeared to be covered by the Trust and in any case was the Trust still valid? Who were the current owners of the land; had the Church acquired any rights resulting from its continued use of part of the land? There was also the added complication that HCC had recognised the whole of the triangular grassed area claimed by the Church as highway.

Following the meeting, the writer gathered together all the available information on the Public Walk and presented it in a report to the Town Council in June 1999.

The 30-page report was based on material from Hampshire Record Office, the Broadlands collection at Southampton University, TVBC archives in Andover and the local history society, the LTVAS Group. It reviewed the history of the land and refuted the Church's solicitor's claim to part of it (the grassed area between the two vicarages). It also recommended that the Town Council should seek independent legal advice to determine the interests of all the parties involved.

The Hampshire Association of Parish and Town Councils (HAPTC)
The report was dicussed at a Town Council meeting in April 2000 where it was decided to seek legal advice from HAPTC which was available to them at no cost. In June 2000 the Town Clerk, the writer and Ted Mason (a lawyer with experience of charitable trusts, village greens and highway land status) met with the honorary legal adviser to HAPTC. In his view, the Trust did subsist and he proposed that the Town Council should write to the Church Authorities and to TVBC asking them to acknowledge it.

However, the situation was complicated by the fact that only parts of the original Public Walk were covered by the available documents (the 1826 conveyances from Young and Sharp to the Corporation) and these parts were not very well defined. During the following year, this problem was further researched and discussed with the TVBC lawyer in an attempt to get a better understanding of what took place when the old and the new vicarages were built.

2001 – The Charity Commission intervenes
In May 2001, a discussion with the Charity Commission showed that the Public Walk was a matter of interest to them despite the time that had elapsed since the Trust was set up. It was decided to ask the Commission formally if it considered the statements in the 1826 conveyances were sufficient to constitute a Charitable Public Trust.

Their reply on 21st November 2001 was surprising. Citing legal precedents, the Charity Commission not only considered the Public Walk to be a Charitable Trust but they had also written to TVBC requiring them to register it with them!

Subsequent correspondence from the Legal Services department in TVBC to Romsey Town Council explained that TVBC had no choice about registering the land with the Charity Commission as it was required under Statutory Powers imposed on them by the Commission. However, the Charity Commission's role does not extend to defining the boundaries of the land involved; that is a matter for the Trustees. Hence, the first thing the Council had to do was to define the boundaries and to register the land with the Land Registry. Following that, the council's legal department wrote; *"The land subject to the Trust will be transferred to a charity as required by the Charity Commissioner"*.

Land Registry involvement

TVBC carried out careful measurements of the land and using the 1826 conveyances determined the extent of the land governed by the Trust. This was no easy task as the old conveyances were very poorly drafted and contained some obvious mistakes such as defining a small but critical area (of 7¼ square perches) as being located to the north (rather than south) of the boundary which placed it on neighbouring property! This was clearly a crass mistake in view of the fact that the church and its weathervane alongside gave a fair indication of which way was north. But such mistakes provide a rich feeding ground for lawyers!

It will be remembered that in 1826, the Corporation had sold some land to Young and Sharp and had then bought it back again at the instigation of Lord Palmerston. In order to make the Public Walk into a rectangular shape, they had also bought two smaller pieces of land from Young. From a legal point of view, it is only land that was purchased in 1826 that can be described as the Public Walk and Pleasure Ground although clearly the whole rectangular area was intended to be used for that purpose. Consequently, the charitable trust only covers parts of the rectangular area which are shown hatched in the sketch.

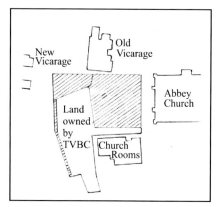

By April 2003, the Land Registry had carried out its own survey and was preparing to serve notice to the Church. When it did so, the Church's solicitors immediately lodged an objection to the registration on the grounds that it claimed ownership of part of the land. Extensive correspondence between the three parties ensued until November 2003 when the Land Registry at Weymouth declared that it was unable to resolve ownership and was sending the papers to the Registry's London office in Chancery Lane where a special team would be set up to resolve the differences between the Church and the Council or, alternatively, refer the matter to the Court of Chancery. Instead of that, in February 2004, the Registry's London Office referred the matter to its Peterborough Office!

Argument at the time largely centred on the location of the 7¼ sq. perches of land (the top left-hand area in the sketch) which in the 1826 deeds had been mistakenly placed on the wrong side of the boundary. Since the Church had no hard evidence of ownership and the true position of this piece of land (in the corner between the new and the old vicarages) was blatantly obvious, it is hard to see why the Land Registry should make such a meal of it. The situation recalled that in 1985 when a reader pointedly wrote (page 39) to the *Romsey Advertiser* asking *"What is the collusion between Church and State?"*.

TVBC goes to Chancery

It was not until February 2005 that the Land Registry finally reached a decision. Their decision was that they had refused to register the charity as title to the land because of the Church's objections and because the Church was claiming ownership of part of the land. Furthermore, the Land Registry directed TVBC to commence proceedings in the High Court of Chancery before the 30th of April 2005. So after a couple of years 'consideration' in three different Land Registry offices, it was now urgent that the matter be decided in Chancery! TVBC had no option in the matter. The Land Registry has the power to make them do that just as the Charity Commission had the power to direct them to register the charity. One felt a certain sympathy for the council.

TVBC duly appointed a London solicitor and a barrister to act for them as their very specialised knowledge is essential in such cases. But both Council and Church were anxious to avoid costly litigation so they continued to negotiate throughout 2005.

On the 6th of January 2006 TVBC registered with the Land Registry all the areas of trust land that were not disputed by the Church. The title number is HP 666721 and TVBC are named as "trustees of the charity known as Romsey Public Walk and Pleasure Ground" so the Trust had been formally recognised. In the following month, the Chancery case was temporarily stopped to give Church and Council yet more time for discussion. Aware of the needs of the Church and local people, the council was planning to create some new car parking spaces alongside the Public Walk which was to be restored as park land.

The PCC goes to Chancery and councillors intervene
On the 26th of October 2007, the PCC (Parochial Church Council) issued a claim (1) (number 7SOO5793) against TVBC to ownership of the land adjoining the church hall or, alternatively, the right to park motor vehicles there. Unlike the previous claims to own the triangular grassed area that were without substance, the claim to ownership of the tarmac area adjoining the church hall was based on 'adverse possession'. This is a rule in which a person or body can claim ownership of land if they have 'occupied' it for more than 12 years. The problem was that other people had also used the land for parking and legal opinion was that the chances of success in this claim were very slim.

The council responded to the claim in a document titled 'Defence and Counterclaim' (2) which rejected the PCC claim point by point. These are publicly available documents which are valuable because they summarise the history of negotiations between Church and Council seen from both points of view. Importantly, in explaining how these ceased at one point the TVBC document notes that use of the land as a car park "would or might" constitute a breach of the Trust.

Early in 2008 local councillors intervened and instructed council officers to reach agreement with the PCC allowing cars to continue to be parked on the land. The planned court hearing for the 31st of March was stayed to give the two parties more time to reach agreement. This instruction from councillors caused a problem in the TVBC legal department. Those working on the case for 10 years or so with the ultimate objective of restoring the land to the trust and landscaping it to provide a better setting for the church must have seen all their work being wasted but the instruction from the councillors could not be ignored. Now they were being instructed to allow cars to be parked on the land having stated in court that there was a risk, if not a certainty, of infringing the Trust.

Once again in a cleft stick situation, some very clever footwork would be required by the council to balance these conflicting requirements in such a way that it would be approved by the Charity Commission.

Church and Council went into secret session.

The Freedom of Information Act and the Attorney General
At this point, the small group of us who had been involved in the case for over 12 years became concerned. The last time that Church and council had gone into secret session (in 1985 – see page 39) the result had been disastrous. The agreement reached involved the council selling part of the Trust land to the Church: this was in breach of the Trust and, later, in 2006, they had to retrieve it. Additionally, there was the concern that the hearing in Chancery had taken no proper account of the Trust.

We wrote letters to the TVBC legal department and to the Charity Commission asking, via the Freedom of Information Act, to try to find out what was going on but both replied they could say nothing whilst Court proceedings were underway. We wrote to the High Court of Chancery to complain that the Trust was being overlooked in the proceedings between Church and Council. The judge replied saying that we should write to the Attorney General, as it was his role to protect charities in this situation. In our letter to the Attorney General we summarised the history of the Public Walk, pointing out that the Church had tried to gain control of the land eight times since the Trust came into effect and we asked him to intervene. He replied saying he would investigate the matter with Council, Church and the Charity Commission and let us know the outcome. That moment has still to come.

Nunc ubi stamus?

So what do we have to show for 12 years' work? Well, the charitable trust initiated by Lord Palmerston is now recognised by the Charity Commission. All of the land shown in the sketch on page 45 is now registered with the Land Registry and those parts of it governed by the Trust are noted in the Title.

The chance of having the land restored to an attractive garden with car parking alongside, which seemed so close at one point when a sponsor was found for the work, has probably passed by. At the time of writing, the Council is in secret negotiation with the Church that is not even a beneficiary of the Trust. Any agreement they reach will certainly be legal but will it be ethical and will it be to the benefit of the people of Romsey as a whole?

Whatever the outcome, Romsonians can now be quite sure that they own this piece of land and the council are merely the Trustees. So the council has no right to treat the land as its own. When the new vicarage was built in 1985, it was clear that people cared about this sensitive part of the town and they will want it to be treated with respect. Their right to demand this is now established

1,2. Copies of these documents can be found in the Hampshire Record Office reference 179A07.

Footnote:

The author has been kept informed by the council, although only in outline, of proceedings over the last 10 years for two reasons; firstly because of his interest in carrying out continued historical research and secondly because he may have been needed as a witness in a Chancery case. Sensitive issues were never discussed and the council lawyer, a man of remarkable tenacity and dedication, always acted with the utmost discretion as would be expected.

Appendix

The following is a transcription of a document found in the Hampshire Record Office written when Avery Moore was trying to establish a case for purchasing part of the Public Walk from the Corporation. It was found among other papers on the same subject:

"Copy of Trusts in which land vested in Corporation of Romsey is held

Upon Trust to permit the said Land to be used at all times for ever hereafter as a Public Walk or Pleasure Ground, for all peaceable and orderly persons, so that such persons do confine themselves to, and not deviate from, the Gravel Walks now made upon the said Land. Provided always that it shall be competent for the said Mayor Alderman and Burgesses their Successors and Assignees and their officers at all times to remove and put out all riotous and disorderly persons, and all persons committing any nuisance, doing any damage, or occasioning any disturbance injury or inconvenience whatsoever in or upon the said Land or any part thereof. And for that purpose to lock up and fasten the Gates belonging to the said Land for such times or seasons as the said Mayor Aldermen and Burgesses and their Successors or Assignees shall think proper – it being the intention and meaning of these presents that the said Land shall be only used as a Public Walk or Pleasure Ground by peaceable and orderly persons."

"…a spot of green tastefully laid out with shrubs and flowers…"
– Mudies 'Hampshire' describing the Public Walk in 1840.

ISBN 978-0-9563311-0-6

9 780956 331106